T0129320

Once Lost, Now Found

Billy Lee

authorHOUSE®

AuthorHouse™
1663 Liberty Drive
Bloomington, IN 47403
www.authorhouse.com
Phone: 1 (800) 839-8640

Scripture quotations marked NKJV are taken from the New King James Version. Copyright © 1982 by Thomas Nelson, Inc. Used by permission. All rights reserved.

Published by AuthorHouse   06/13/2018

ISBN: 978-1-5462-4603-9 (sc)
ISBN: 978-1-5462-4602-2 (e)

Library of Congress Control Number: 2018906709

Print information available on the last page.

This book is printed on acid-free paper.

Contents

Purpose

THE DEVIL THOUGHT HE had me, but I am out of his hands. Psalm 8:2 states, "Out of the mouths of babes and nursing infants, you have ordained strength, because of your enemies, that you may silence the enemy and the avenger."

I sincerely and prayerfully wrote this book with the hope that it may be an inspiration and encouragement to others who are struggling to overcome their addiction problems and that through my testimony, they will become the "Victor" without a lot of grief.

REFERENCE

ALL SCRIPTURAL REFERENCES ARE from the New King James Version of the Holy Bible.

DEDICATION

THIS BOOK IS DEDICATED to my mother and my family. My mother did her very best to instill within me, the Love of God from an early childhood. I know she prayed many nights that she would not be awakened by an unfavorable telephone call, which could have been news of my tragic death. I thank my brother, who is also a minister. We have been blessed through our close relationship and many family experiences God has given us an opportunity to see a glimpse of the end result for this life.

I would like to thank my wife, for her encouragement and support as well as my three daughters and grand and great grandchildren, 32 and counting.

I also dedicate this book to my Pastor and church family. Had it not been for them, I would not be where I am right now in my faith, the Word of God and Christian fellowship.

I am thankful and grateful to my Austin race director and friend. He helped me with my attitude towards the Veterans Administration (VA) and the military when I had lost all respect for them. With his encouragement and support, I was blessed to be a part of the first Honor Flight from Austin to Washington, D. C. that allowed me to visit the Vietnam Veteran's wall. It was there that my vision was revived to run marathons in honor of my comrades who gave their lives for this country.

I thank my Veterans Administration counselor, who helped me with my Post Traumatic Stress Disorder (PTSD). She also assisted me with locating my comrades, giving me the opportunity to visit three of eight gravesites of men who were killed on February 1, 1968, at the TAT Offense. I was able to share the scripture from Ezekiel 37:1-13 with their bones in Los Angeles, Chicago and Austin.

I would like to thank my running coach, and my running family. Without their support, I would not be running at the level that I am running now.

I would also like to thank the Catholic Diocese, Ministry and the many Christian friends that I have met as I traveled on this Emmaus Road. I have been greatly encouraged by them to keep "Pressing On".

We all need encouragement and support and everybody needs somebody. God designed the body with two arms and two legs to support the body. The people listed in this dedication have provided a similar type of support to me and for that I am grateful.

Thanks to my Writing/ Publishing Consultant and Editor.

MY EARLY LIFE

My name is Billy Lee, but my friends and family call me Bill. I was born in Austin, Texas and I am the youngest of two sons. I attended Austin Public Schools and grew up in a single parent home.

I remember very little about my dad because he left us when I was only 2 ½ years old. As a young child I remember my family moving a lot, going from house to house. We lived with my grandmother for a while and then with my aunt, who lived across the street from a Catholic Church. The Catholic Church is also where I attended Pre-Kindergarten and Kindergarten. At the time, I was not sure why we were moving around so much and I do not remember my dad being there at the time.

Being a single parent, my mother was determined to do the best for us and give us a stable life. She would work 2-3 jobs to make ends meet. In addition to working multiple jobs, she also returned to school to receive a college education and become a school teacher. She never accepted food stamps or welfare because she believed God would provide for our family. She did what she had to do to survive and by her faith and trusting in the Lord, we survived. My mother kept us in church. During church service, she would give us money for the offering and instead of putting the money in the offering plate, I would go across the street to a friend's house and indulge in a dice game.

The greatest evangelist I have ever known was my mother. My mother was a God-fearing woman. I never woke up to see a man in her house. She held on to her faith and endured the challenges that were before her and pressed forward. She never stopped praying and always spoke in love. She suffered with great patience in dealing with my problems and never got in the way of my addictions. She always gave God the glory, regardless of the situation. My mother became the first "overcomer" for my eyes to see and her lifestyle has definitely been a testimony to me.

My mother allowed my brother and I the opportunity to attend kindergarten at the Holy Cross Catholic Church, while she worked two jobs. We would have fun at school. My mom would give us peanut butter and jelly sandwiches for lunch and during snack time, I would go and throw my sandwiches over a fence to some chickens because I did not like peanut butter at that time. We would also take breaks and naps at school. I remember one day, while napping, I urinated on myself. I saw the urine going down my leg and to the floor. I was scared and shaking, thinking that others could see what was happening. That was my first experience and memory of fear. Sister Mary, one of the teachers, saw me and came over to comfort me. She told me that it was alright and that sometimes children have accidents. Sister Mary's words gave me confidence and let me know that I should never be afraid.

After moving out of my aunt's house, we moved to the projects. Each day, my brother and I would meet my mom at the bus stop. My mom would always tell us to always stay together and not to get on the bus without seeing her arm out of the window. One day, while we were walking down the street, I saw a bus and ran and got on without waiting for my brother. This particular bus did not go back to the projects, it went downtown. On the last stop, the bus driver, who was a white man, told me, a black 6 year old boy, that it was the end of the route and that I had to get off the bus. So I got off the bus, not knowing anything about traffic lights or crossing the street. I almost got hit several times, by cars, trying to cross the street. I kind of knew the area, because my mom would take us downtown periodically to go to stores and to pay bills. When I started walking up, I saw the Capitol building, which leads to the street where the bus would always passed by. And I remembered that particular bus would turn right on that street, going to the east side. So I walked up the street and arrived back at Catholic Church, but no one was there. Then I walked down towards the next street and I saw a woman walking towards me, wearing a black dress. It was my mother and she had been looking for me. I started crying when I saw her. She told me that it was alright and took me home. I asked where was my brother, and she said he was already at home.

We stayed in the projects, with some other families that also lived there. They would have parties frequently in the area. I learned a lot and saw many things living in the projects. They use to have dances in the offices at the projects and often fights would start. One night, while hanging out with friends across the street from a dance party, I think I saw this man with his arm hanging off his body, like it had been cut off. I saw a lot of blood, but I never really knew what actually happened to him.

We were considered the hoodlums of the neighborhood and the Park area. One day, when I was playing with a few guys, a boy started pushing me around. I was kind of scared until I saw my mother and then I got the confidence and courage to fight him. Eventually, I became friends with the guy. I did a lot of fighting back then, contrary to the clean cut or good kids in the neighborhood. In our day, our mischievous acts included throwing rocks and breaking picture windows of people's houses, unlike drive-by shootings that take place today. We would see a house with large picture windows and would throw the rocks at the windows and run.

There was a neighbor, an older man that worked at the neighborhood store, who would give me candy and cigarettes. I found out this man was the devil because he end up molesting me. I was in the first grade when this happened. This is also when I started smoking. I had a half-brother who taught me how to fight and after that incident, I started fighting and taking up for myself, being a thug. There was another incident that happened and my brother forced me to fight, but I didn't want to fight. My brother told me that if I didn't fight, he would kick my ass. When the man who molested me, found out about my half-brother, he stopped messing with me. He knew my brother had a fighting reputation. Eventually, the man that molested me moved and I didn't have any problems with him afterwards. I didn't tell anyone what had happened to me. It took me years to overcome that experience and I drew closer to God after that. Through every life experience, I could hear the Word of God, even though I did not really know Him or understand, my conscience kept convicting me.

I was about 9 years old when I saw my friends from the neighborhood doing the same thing that happened to me.

That is when I clammed up and really got silent. I starting fighting more because my trust was broken. I thought if my friends knew what happened to me, would they treat me differently? I made a blood oath with myself that no one would ever hurt me again.

We stayed on 'the hill' in the projects where some neighborhood kids and I would hang out. Hanging out around the projects, at that time, you could not go under the hill depending on where you lived. It was like a gang territory thing. You could not to get caught in another area.

When I started the sixth grade, I became withdrawn. I didn't have anyone to talk to and my mom was always working. I did, however, have a friend who stayed next door to us. When I would run away from home, he would let me stay with him because his dad worked nights and would not have known I had been there. While my mom was at work, I would leave my friend's house and go eat at home. I had a lot of friends who, when I think about it now, were not really friends. I would consider them more as associates. I kind of disassociated myself from them because of my paranoia. In the eighth grade, I started meeting guys from different neighborhoods and other schools. I began associating with the "bad crowd" because I wanted to be known as a tough guy. I did not want anyone to ever hurt me again. I was a walking time bomb, due to being abused and assaulted and I became known as a fighter. I would come home when I wanted to, just running the streets, doing drugs and alcohol.

In school, I was passed from grade to grade. I attended Junior High and from there I went to High School. Attending High School was the worst mistake of my life because I was a radical young black teen attending a newly integrated school and I was not ready for integration. I got into a confrontation with the Vice Principal at High School and was expelled.

I ended up getting into more trouble with other guys afterwards.

In high school, I didn't really trust anyone. I became rebellious, drinking alcohol, smoking marijuana and doing drugs. When I was in the 9th grade, one of my classmates, who was a female, called me a black bastard. Back in those days words really hurt and I did not really have anyone to encourage me and let me know that I was not a bastard kid. One day, I happened to pick her name for a Christmas gift exchange. I went to a drug store with a cousin of mine to get her a gift. I told my cousin that I was going to get her some dogfood as a Christmas gift, for calling me a black bastard. He was buying dog food for someone else as well. I came back from the store and put the dogfood, which was wrapped, under the Christmas tree. I kept the actual gift I had also bought in my pocket until it was time to present the gift to her. When she opened the gift, she saw the bull dog face on the packaging and started crying. I felt bad in my heart so I gave her the actual gift I bought, but she did not want it. My teacher came into the room and I got into it with him because of that incident. I saw that he was coming towards me to attack me, so I pulled my knife on him. The Vice Principal came in and broke us up. I ended up in the principal's office, where I got expelled. I was sent home several times because of the incident with the dog food. Every time the principal saw me in the hall, he would call me into his office and expel me. I couldn't go back to school until my mother brought me back.

One day I used my mom's car to drive to different high schools to fight other students and teachers. On that day, while driving from school to school, I ended up at our High School and got into a fight in the cafeteria. When my friends and I were leaving, we were stopped by the police. While we were in the car, I told my friends that I was going to start a fight with the police so they could get away. Only one friend had the courage to get out and run. We ended up going to jail and later taken to the juvenile detention center. I was kicked out of all the public schools in Austin because of my misbehavior. In spite of my mother's constant teachings and admonishments, I became a high school dropout in the 10th grade.

In 1964, I was released from juvenile detention and sent to live with my dad in California. I was 16 years old at the time. It was different living with my dad. He really didn't know how to raise kids, so I ended up hustling on my own. I was doing a lot of gambling, drinking and drugs. I would shoot crooked dice as a side hustle. My dad was a loan shark and he would loan people money that they would have to pay back. When they came to our house to pay on their loans, I would convince them to shoot a little dice with me and that was my hustle then.

I had older step brothers and sisters that I would hang out with, while staying with my dad. Growing up, I would always try to find people who had the same mind set or mentality that I did. I had an "I don't care" attitude because my trust was broken. Living a life without trusting people was a very difficult life for me to adjust to.

I really didn't have an interest in going to school. I preferred to hang out in the streets. I continued to get into trouble and pick fights with people. I met other groups of guys while in California and we started hanging out. We eventually became active in a local basketball group at the Boys and Girls Club. One day, we went to a neighborhood school to play basketball and one of the players, who was a white guy, kept elbowing me in the side. He just kept elbowing me and I started to become agitated so much that my friends had to calm me down. But when we went into the showers, I jumped him. I ended up going to jail for that incident because I had cut his eye and broke his nose. My dad had to come pick me up. When he arrived, he told me the next time I got into a fight, he was going to kick my ass because he didn't want to pay a fine to spend his money. He changed his mind about that when he saw the size of the guy, when we were at the courthouse. He then smiled at me and seemed kind of proud that I was able to defend myself against a guy twice my size.

While I was living with my dad, I saw him get baptized and that is when we started going to church. At that time, I was just going to church just to meet girls. The type of biblical teaching available today was not available to me back then. I got involved with the Pastor's daughter and she became pregnant. Every Sunday, the Pastor would preach a sermon pertaining to fathers and sons and people letting their daughters get pregnant and not being responsible parents. He would call my dad all the time to talk to him about it. One particular time, he called my dad to talk to him and my dad cursed him out over the phone. After he cursed him out, my dad told him that he would kick his ass all over the pulpit if he preached that same sermon he had been preaching each Sunday. The next Sunday morning, my dad woke me up to get ready for church. I told him that I was not going to church. But my step mom persuaded me to go because she knew how my dad would react. My dad also told me that if I didn't ever go to church again, I was going that day. We arrived at church and when the Pastor got up to preach his sermon, he preached a new sermon! I believe it was because my dad had threatened him and told him he would kick his ass. My dad looked at me and laughed because he knew why the Pastor had changed his sermon. That experience turned me away from the church and preachers. Regarding me and my girlfriend, my dad said that I was too young to marry, so I ran away from home. I wanted to marry her because I found out she was pregnant. When I got to her house my dad called the police and I was taken from her house to juvenile detention. A week later I got a letter from my girlfriend telling me that she was getting married to an older guy in the church. This was another turning point in my life.

After that incident, my dad got into an argument with my step mom and they separated shortly afterwards. My dad eventually got into another relationship. The woman he was involved with purposely tried to incite an argument between my dad and I. She told my dad that I was not scared of him, and that I could whoop him. One day I was getting ready to go out and my dad came in and approached me about what his girlfriend said. He started walking towards me to hit me and I went up under him, picked him up and threw him on the bed. I drew back to hit him, but I remembered my mom told me to respect your elders. So I ran and went to my uncle's house. He brought me back to the house and told my dad that I was going to work with him to raise money for a bus ticket back home. Working with my uncle, I was able to get enough money to come back to Austin.

In Austin, I became deeply involved in crime. I was still radical and getting into more trouble. I would run away from home and the police would have to search for and chase after me. I had a little hiding place that I would go to in the woods. The police were chasing me one day and one of the police officers pointed a gun at me and told me to halt or he'll blow my brains away. But I cursed him out and ran. A few weeks later they were chasing me again and they caught me that time. My mom told the police to bring me home. After that incident, I started mingling in with guys, hanging out in clubs and doing more drugs.

Failure to communicate can cause a person to grow bitter, indignant, and confused. I became all of those things, because of the experiences of my youth. I became withdrawn, so I didn't relate to a lot of people. I started hanging out on the streets with women and I became experienced with prostitutes. I would see guys strung out on drugs and I would tell them that they were weak because they were hooked on drugs. A guy inside one of the drug houses told me, "You just keep on hanging around here and you'll get into doing drugs yourself." One day I was sick with a cold or what I thought was a cold and a guy told me, "You are not sick." He told me to come into the house so he could give me a "fix" (of drugs). He said that it would calm me down. That was the beginning of my addiction. I became strung out on drugs at an early age and became a run-away, drug dealer, drug user, panderer, thief and robber.

The last time I got caught by the police, I was sent to court. While I was in court, they gave me a choice of either going to prison or into the military. I chose the military for four years. I was about 18 years old at the time. I knew my life was in trouble and I thought that if I went into the military there would be hope to make a better man of myself. I joined the Marines and I believed this was a good opportunity for me to start over. When I arrived, there were a few minorities in boot camp with me and there was also prejudice that I didn't notice at the time, only because we had a black gunnery sergeant. I was fortunate because I was chosen, by the gunnery sergeant, to be a squad leader. I was very fortunate to make rank out of boot camp. In Boot Camp, they would train us with two words, "Yes sir!" and "Kill!" In other words, we were trained to show respect and kill the enemy. I made Private First Class after boot camp. We had to go to the rifle range to qualify or we would have to start all over in boot camp. The sergeant would make us stand in line as part of drills and say "right side" or "left side" and we would each get slapped. If he called right, then the man you were facing would slap you and if he called the left, you would slap him. He knew the slapping was getting to me because it was a white guy in front of me. The next time he said "left", I "downed" the guy. I hit him pretty hard. I had to go through 12 weeks of boot camp. When it was the 10th week, we had to qualify at the rifle range. When I couldn't qualify on the first day, the sergeant made me wallow in the sand pit that was wet with water, and I had to sleep all night in that situation. The next morning, I still couldn't qualify and the sergeant gave me a heavy M14 rifle to hold, while my arms were stretched out. He told me that if I dropped it, he would kick my ass. The next morning, I finally qualified for the range. After boot camp, they gave us 30 days leave, before giving us orders to go to Vietnam. I married my wife in October 1967 and after we were married, I returned to basic infantry training. They gave me orders to go to Vietnam, but I wanted to stay in the States until my child was born and then I would go anywhere they wanted me to go, to live or die. My commander told me that I could not stay in the States because I had to prove something to them. I got mad and said, "I don't have nothing to prove to you."

Since I was not able to stay in the States, I went Absent Without Leave (AWOL). I left for Mexico and stayed there for a while and then went to Oakland. When my dad found out I went AWOL, he told me I was a deserter and that I should turn myself in. That was the only encouragement he ever gave me; it was the only good advice I ever received from him. I really wanted to make something good out of my life, but when I went to turn myself in, I got court marshaled and sent to lock up until I got orders to go to Vietnam. I wanted to serve, but I also wanted to see and spend time with my wife and daughter.

On my flight to Vietnam I met Kenneth. We were friends but not really close. We just happened be in the same situation at the same time, so we ended up talking to each other. We would argue with each other all the time, as two brothers would, then we would go hang out at the local clubs and get high. He would always try to correct me and we would just argue back and forth. One time he told me that the next time we get orders, he hoped that we would be sent different places. When we got our orders, we were both sent to the same place, in the same squad team, same fire team. This was in December 1967, when I was about 19 years old. We arrived in Da Nang, Vietnam and we were walking through the Barracks. A grenade was thrown on the tier and I froze and Kenneth froze. Another man picked up the grenade and threw it over the fence, but it did not go off. It was considered a "dud". The next morning the grenade went off and that is when I knew God was with us. They had a saying in "the Bush" in Vietnam, you had a 50/50 chance of staying alive after 90 days, a 60/40 chance after five months, 70/30 chance after seven months, 80/20 chance after nine months, and a 90/10 chance after 11 months, then you were likely to survive because you knew how to survive in the jungle "bush".

We were in our platoon and this racist corporal would put us in difficult, horrible detail all the time. We were like shit birds to him, in the platoon, and that was how they treated us. Every detail that was given to us was difficult to do and it stripped us of our character. Kenneth and I were just trying to make it through our time in the military and get back home, so we did what was told of us. We were sweeping through a village one day with our Point man, Pete. There were two more Marines behind Pete, and then myself, the fourth man, the radio man and sixth man, who was the Lieutenant. Kenneth was the seventh man and we were all going through this village on a small trial. A land mine was hit and I fell down and Kenneth was standing up yelling. Pete was yelling "Help, help." I thought I had a concussion because I could not see too well at first. When I turned to look at Kenneth, I saw he had a hole in his chest the size of a large grapefruit. I told him to get down. Air strikes finally came in and everything was calm. We got pulled to another area and after a while it became peaceful. We were trying to get the casualty count, but my main concern was Kenneth. And we went around for our casualty count and there was a navy medic there, whom we would exchange marijuana for opium or morphine. We would give him marijuana and he would give us morphine and opium. He was with another squad, and we went around to see who was injured or hurt and the navy medic, who we called "Doc", was sitting hunched over with a pistol to his head. I wasn't sure if he had shot himself or not. I went back and started smoking and laughing with Kenneth. We talked a little bit until the helicopter came. The helicopter arrived and they began taking away all the wounded. I helped Kenneth onto the chopper and told him he had a "million dollar wound" because that is what they called it when you got shot. Before he left I told him that I would see him again, when we get out of the military. Two days later, the captain told us to take this hill and we would not have to worry about the wounded and that kind of worried me. While going through the fields, looking out to the hills, I saw smoke coming from a rocket, so I yelled "Incoming!" And the rocket hit in front of me. Shrapnel was coming towards me and as I turned to get away from the explosion, I was hit. I was medevac'd to a hospital for a few days. It took me 12 days to get back to the unit and when I arrived, I found out Kenneth had died. I felt like they let him die because I was told that he lived 9 days and he seemed ok when I left him. I believe he died because of the racism that was going on back then. I only knew Kenneth for 60 days, before he passed away. During those 60 days, I began to open up and became comfortable sharing how I felt about life. We also became really close during that time. When he ate, I ate and when he watched, I slept. We both talked about our families and got to know each other. We didn't get to really know each until we got inland in Vietnam for 60 days. We eventually became close friends. I think those were best years of my life, because I was more relaxed and we both treasured each other's friendship. His death turned me away from the military. I went AWOL into the villages to get away. I was 20 years old at the time.

I began writing letters to Congress in 1968, explaining that I wanted to get out of Vietnam. The rule back then was if you had two 48 hour wounds, they kept you from going into field again. We got in another fire fight and I was leading a bunch of new recruits who had just arrived to Vietnam. They were anxious and scared. I was told to bring the squad up to another location, but they would not move, which is when I got wounded trying to push the squad up under the fire fight that we were in. After that experience, I told them that I was through fighting. I let them know that I was serious by going AWOL. After I wrote congress and went AWOL a friend of mine came looking for me while I was AWOL in the village and he told me they had orders for me to get out of Vietnam in 48 hours. Eventually, I was sent to Okinawa in May of 1968. I got into a fight with a white guy because he said something I did not like. I went to the "Brig" because of that incident I lost my stripes. I had to stay there until I received orders to leave to go to Guam in June 1968. They sent me to Guam to finish the rest of my tour of duties which was 13 months.

In Guam, I was assigned to the Marine Corps barracks. I began hanging out with radical guys and we picked up two sailors and robbed them. Guam was a small island, so there were not too many places to hide. We ended up going jail for that crime and had to wait to be court martialed. We were held for aggravated robbery that could have resulted in 27 years in prison. When we got out of the Brig, our attorney told us that we would have to do something to make what we had done right so we would stay out of trouble. .I thought when I got out of the Brig, my sentence could be reduced if I could do something good. So when I got out of the Brig, I joined the football team to keep me out of trouble. I made a name for myself playing football. When we finally went to court, we found out that they had dropped the case. I really do not know why they dropped the case, but looking back, I believe God has been blessing me all along even in that situation, keeping me all along.

We didn't get a good welcome at home when we came back from Vietnam because they considered us baby killers and such. I didn't know at the time, but my wife told my daughter that there was something different about me when I came back and I had not realized that. I came back to the states and took my family to California for a little while.

During our flight home, I met this guy and he invited me to stay with him and his sister for the night, because we had a layover in Los Angeles, then we would leave the next morning. When we landed in Los Angeles that night, she threw a party for her brother and we were drinking and partying and ended up running out of liquor, so we went to the store to get more. I also wanted some pig's feet to eat and was hoping I could buy that at the store as well. While we were inside the store, I was looking for my pig's feet and I looked up and saw a black brother robbing the store. He said, "All I want is the white man's money". I tried to explain to him that we had just come from Vietnam and asked him not to shoot us. He then walked us to the back room and left. After he closed the door, it was quiet. We didn't hear anything for a while. I walked out to the front of the store and the robber had left. I bought my pig's feet and I did not go outside of the house anymore after that experience was enough for me. This was in December 1968.

My relationship with my wife didn't last too long, because I started doing drugs again. We would experience highs and lows in our relationship. We got into an argument and she wanted out of the relationship. I went to sleep one night and woke up and she was gone. I saw the yellow pages open to the page to call a cab. I went outside of the apartment to ask if anyone had seen a cab in the area. I found out my wife had called for a yellow cab to come pick her up and take her to the bus station. I drove to bus station and asked if someone had seen a woman and child board a bus and asked where the bus was going. A clerk told me that the bus that she boarded was going to Texas and had a layover in San Diego. I drove to San Diego, found my wife and daughter and brought them back to the house. I told my commander what had happened and he gave me orders to take my family home. So I travelled back to Texas with my family. After that incident, I began my military duties. All Vietnam Veterans were having a hard time because all we wanted to do was party, going from San Diego to Los Angeles on the weekends. But we had problems getting into clubs because we were under 21. We became very radical. In Vietnam, we could go to clubs and drink with no questions ask. But after defending our country and going back to the States, we could not go to clubs and we thought that was a double standard.

In 1970, I got an early release with an honorable discharge because they were wanting to get the bad apples out the military. I didn't realize until later, when I applied for food stamps, that it was easy for you to get on welfare or unemployment. That was my whole life, just getting over on people. I was wrestling with my identity since my childhood and that affected me until I got saved. I didn't have a good relationship with people because of the abuse I experienced as a young child. I just didn't have trust in people. After the military I got into a whole life of crime of stealing and robbing and just trying to get over. I left Los Angeles and came back to Texas and continued to hustle. I started selling drugs when I came back to Austin, but I was my best customer. I never made any money, because I would shoot it up myself. I got back to Texas and tried to relate with my mom and family, but no one could understand me. I didn't communicate too well with them and I was so ashamed of my past. It was easy for me to hide by hanging around with people who were doing the same thing. My communication was not too good with people and my mom would always tell me that I needed to open up. God has been with me my whole life and I thank God for my mom praying for me. I knew that there was a God, but I did not know God. I know that I should have been dead many times over, from shoot outs in the streets, war and overdoses. So God has kept me for a reason, and I am still not sure what it is. But until I find out, I will go on and be that light and encourager for other people.

After moving back to Texas, my relationship with my wife did not work out, so we got divorced. I was trying to be a player. I ended up getting into a relationship with another woman who played both ends, she was a prostitute and a sex fling for the police officer. I would get harassed because she was involved with one of the police officers. They would always pull me over to harass me. So I pulled her aside one day and told her to stay away from that cop she was involved with. The cop came to our apartment one night and he said he was going to take her in because she was on probation, but didn't have warrant. I didn't know she was on probation. I told him she is not going anywhere with you, but when he asked her if she wanted to go, she said yes, so I let her go. Later, I got a call from her saying she was being booked at the police station for violation of probation and she wanted me to wait for her until she got out of jail. I did not want to wait for her, so I got back into the streets. A guy was selling drugs for me, who was short on money and I went to his house to get it. I started beating on the door and his wife called the police and told them that some guys were trying to rob her house. So when she told me that I went down the street and I left but came back a little later after I saw the police car. By that time the police had come and it was the same policeman that had been harassing me. He took me to jail. After I got out of jail in 1971, pending my trial, I went to Houston for the Methadone drug program, awaiting my court date there at the Veterans Administration. I then met another woman while in the program and she invited me to stay with her. We got into a relationship and that kept me out of prison for a while.

I was in and out of jail in Houston and I also did a lot of stuff and hurt a lot of people. The last time I was in Houston we robbed this drug house and got some jewelry and drugs and then we went to Austin to do another robbery. While in Austin, my homeboy introduced me to a "fence". And after I met with the fence, I showed him the jewelry that I had and he seemed to be interested. I asked my homeboy, after we left, what he wanted if we pulled this robbery off and he said he wanted half of the money. I said that he could not get half of the money, because I had two women with me and we would all get a fourth of the money. He didn't agree to the fourth because he said they were my women. I told him that it didn't matter what they did with their money. They would be taking the same chance I was taking. So I took him to buy some drugs to get him fixed and dropped him off and I told him that we were not going to mess with that. Later on that night we went to rob this fence with the ladies I was hustling with. The guy took us to his safe and when he went to open the safe door one of the ladies flinched and her gun went off and he ended up getting shot. When we left, she let me know that she did not mean to shoot the guy. We left for Taylor to buy more drugs and then we went to rob another drug house that we had been getting the drugs from. We also traveled to Fort Worth and then Oklahoma City.

While in Oklahoma, I ran into a guy that I had met in Los Angeles and he introduced me to some people there, one of which was a drug dealer. I began spying him out and one day I saw him driving down the freeway. I told my lady friend that we were going to get him now. So I told her to go knock on the door, while I hid behind her where he couldn't see me through the peephole. When we went into the house, he ran out of the front door into the front yard, yelling I was trying to kill him. I told the people that were outside that he was a dope dealer and to call the police.

After that we drove to Kansas, robbing and using drugs. We got to Junction, Kansas and I saw a man who I thought was a woman, because He was dressed in drag. I began pursuing him and I couldn't stop because my mind was preoccupied with something else. In the street life, when you're playing the game, your reputation is on the line and you are always worried about your reputation and how you were perceived. I had to continue to pursue the guy dressed in drag to keep my character and reputation as hustler, because a slow dollar is better than no dollar. So we went to a hotel and he wanted me to have relations with him, but I told him I was not ready for that. Since we were in the same room, he could see everything that my lady friend and I were doing. After that, I got paranoid about how he was looking at me. So that morning we left to find another car, but I told him to stay in the room while we went to get some drugs. I told my lady friend that we had to leave and find another car. So we left to find another car and when we returned to the hotel, he was gone. All of his things were out of the room. Then we heard a knock on the door. When I asked who it was, they responded that it was the hotel manager, but it was really the police. The guy in drag had reported us to police, telling them that we were in possession of drugs and guns. They put us both in jail. Even though I was in a new jail, I have always been able to find my way in any jail system. In this particular jail, they had a Diagnostic routine that we had to go through that would keep you there for a week. When people came through there, they would ask what section of the jail or "tank" other inmates were in when they came to Diagnostic Clinic. They would tell everyone not to go to "E" tank, because it was a dangerous tank. Unfortunately, they transferred me to E tank cell block, where there were six people in each cell, which would be about 30 people per tank, in the cell blocks or tank. When I arrived to my cell, I laid down and before I knew, it was time for breakfast the next morning and I realized they had not given me a breakfast tray. So I yelled for them to bring me a tray so I was told by the guard that he had put enough trays in the cell and I had to find it. So I went back to my cell and looked through all the other cells to look for the tray and when I reached the last cell there were about six trays on the floor. It turns out they had put enough trays in the cell area so I let one of the guys know that one of those trays were mine. He looked up at me and gave me a frown and gave me my tray. I got my tray, went back to my cell to eat. One of the guys in my cell told me I have to watch what I was doing. After I had eaten I met a guy who told me to be careful how I do stuff here in this jail. I got back to the day room and I was pacing back and forth in the day room. A guy stopped me to ask why I was in jail and I told him that I had gotten busted at the hotel and that broke the ice with me and them. I got along with them because they knew about me getting busted at the hotel and word had spread that I was the one in the news that was arrested because they found money, drugs and weapons. I got along with them until I was transferred and expedited back to Austin.

I got a glimpse of the Lord, while in prison. I met a guy who would tell me about the Lord and I got hooked on the books of Daniel and Revelation in the Bible. In 1976, there came a time when all I would do is read, pray and study the Bible. One day I had a nervous breakdown because I was kind of confused in my study of the Bible. They were coming to pick up the trays from the cells and they wanted me to get out of the breeze way so they could get the trays, but I would not move. When they opened the door, I came out fighting. They had to put me in a padded cell. Every night I would fight in the padded cell, just kicking and fighting and cursing. And around 3 a.m., there was a guy in the next cell who had come back from Rusk state hospital and he would talk to me every night. And he would say to me, "Brother, I know you are not crazy, but if you keep doing what you are doing, they will send your ass to Rusk and give you the electric shock treatment then you really would be crazy". So I stopped my behavior and sent in a request to talk to the captain of the guards to tell him I was ready to get out of the padded cell. I started studying and reading the Bible again. I had several lawyers, some of whom I had to let go, for various reasons. One lawyer tried to get me to cop out or to confess, and the other one was an alcoholic. All through the court or the trial, the District Attorney would compare me to Hitler. I was given a 60 year sentence and when that happened, I threw my Bible far away because I was mad at God. I was sent to Ramsey unit, in the south of Houston and when I got there the first person I saw was a homeboy of mine. When I saw him, I went over to him and told him I needed a shank or a knife to take care of myself while I was in prison. In prison, it's always good to know people and for people to know you. I had another homeboy who had politician status and he took me under his wing when I started doing my time. This was in 1976, the second time I went to prison. I didn't read my Bible or pray at the time because I was mad at God, but I did everything else a convict could do to pass time. I went on bench warrant for another charge back in Houston and I found out some people had contracts on me there. I was in a cell and a guy was telling me his story and he also shared that another guy had told him about me and my lady friend and that the contract was actually out on us. I became a little paranoid, but God had worked it out for me. I came back to prison, off bench warrant, and started doing time. I was scheduled to do 12 years before parole, but the Ruiz vs. Astelle law was in place to prevent cruel and unusual punishment and overcrowding prison conditions. At the time, they were keeping at least 2-3 prisoners per cell and the Ruiz vs. Astelle law eliminated those jail conditions, giving me an early release. And after 8 years I started praying over my food and made my first parole after nine years. I was not prepared for early release. When I was released, my aunt picked me up. As we were driving down town., I told her to slow down because she was driving too fast. She said I am only going 20 miles per hour. I told her that if she did not slow down, I wanted her to stop and let me out of the car. I finally made it home after nine years.

Shortly after that release I got into the streets and into trouble. On my third release from prison, I was studying and reading my Bible and fasting and praying for almost three years and when I got out of prison I went to Houston and arrived at 10:15 p.m. and at 10:30 p.m. I had a rig in my arm, shooting drugs again at a drug house and it came to my mind about robbing this drug house so I had explained to my friend who got out of prison with me about how we could rob this drug house. The guy who gave me the gun was a previous associate from prison who was staying next door to the drug house and this guy had a gun with one bullet. I was wondering how we could rob the drug house with one bullet. I had a plan but I didn't know that my so called friend that I was running with knew about the plan of robbing. He was to fake an overdose and fall out and they would come to him so that I would be able to get the drop on him. The dealer ran out of the house and I ran after him. Another guy was coming out around the side of the house with a shot gun and I saw a blast from the shot gun and I had a burning in my stomach and it seemed like everything was coming out of my body. I ran out of the yard and fell in a ditch across the street and the spirit told me if you stay here you will die. So I got up from the ditch and ran into some backyards and got into some bushes and that's when the Lord told me to stay here. My associate had double-crossed us and was pretending to be on my side, but he was really not I heard the guys running through the neighborhood and that they knew that they had hit me. I got up and went to call my mom from Houston and I told her a lie about how I had got in to an argument in the club and got shot at. because She asked what was wrong with me and what are you doing, I asked my mother for my ex-wife's phone number and she came to pick me up and when she got there, she said look at you man, you just got out of prison and you are doing this again. She took me to the Greyhound bus station and I came Austin. I went to the hospital and I had a bunch of bruises and puss bumps in my stomach, but I was healed and stayed out of the streets for a month then went right back into to the streets again.

My brother was pastoring a church in Austin and I would use his truck to do crimes, drugs and stealing. The truck belonged to my brother, but he allowed to use it. I had to leave his truck for a period of time. My brother was picked up by the police and put in jail because the truck was traced back to him. I stayed next door to my mom and she came and told me that I was messing up everybody's life because my brother was in jail. I panicked and left for San Antonio in Feb. 1989 with my lady friend. We left with only the clothes on our backs. When we arrived in San Antonio, and there was a freeze there. While in San Antonio I found out that we could get clothes and food from a catholic church. Every time we passed by the Catholic Church, My lady friend would always do "Hail Mary" signs. I asked her why she did "Hail Mary stuff and she wasn't sure why, only that she was raised like that. So I told her from now on, every time you do a "Hail Mary", do one for me too! At the time I was doing a little hustle here and there and we were helping out one another. Then we left San Antonio and went to Houston, still stealing and prostituting. I had been taught at a young age that a slow dollar is better than no dollar when hustling was hard. After being in Houston, we went to Louisiana and stayed at a hotel attempting to make ends meet, working the streets. After staying in Louisiana for a while, we went to New Orleans. When we arrived in New Orleans, we met a guy at the bus station hustling people. I told him that I was a dope fiend trying to make it. And he said, "Why in the hell did I have to find a dope fiend today of all days?" He took us under his wings and introduced us to some other dope fiends that were selling hot items and showed us the ins and outs of New Orleans. After a couple of weeks, we robbed a drug dealer and ended up going to Alabama to continue our hustle. Then we went to Panama City and stayed there a while. From there we went to Tampa, Florida. I had a cousin there and he told me that he didn't want any trouble with the law. I told him that the police were looking for me and I wasn't coming to cause him any trouble. So he gave us some money and my lady friend and I got a hotel room in Tampa. We got into a Methadone program, trying to use the program and work the streets at the same time. After staying in Tampa for a while, we left and went to Los Angeles. I found my daughter's mother and we hung out around there for a while. My lady friend got arrested and I had to stay with my daughter's mother until she got out of jail. We left there and went to Sacramento, California and stayed with my other daughter until we got our own place and a car. And we hustled and stayed there until her court date in Los Angles to appear in court. We had to drive back to Los Angeles for the court date and stayed at a friend's house. Then we went to get some drugs, but got pulled over by the police. While they were frisking my lady friend, I remembered there was a gun under the seat. They found the gun and also found out that I had a warrant in Texas. They put me into the police car and started beating me. This is how I came to understand and relate the Rodney King story. And I began to talk to the Lord and ask him that if he would take my life that I would give it to Him, and I said, Lord, I do not know how to pray but if you take my life, I would give you my life and that is how I came to know the Lord. All my life I had always fought back no matter who it was. If it was police or whoever, I would always fight back. I went to my cell and found a Bible between the commode and the wall and picked it and started reading. They gave me a phone call and I used it to call my daughter in Sacramento to connect with them and she asked me, Dad, you've tried everything, why don't you try Jesus? I told her I did try Jesus. Be that as it may; in doing everything in life, we have to make sure it is right with God first.

TRY JESUS

I SPENT 14 YEARS of my life in prison at four different times, serving one year, nine years, and three year and one year terms. For almost 30 years, my motivation, physically and mentally, was drugs. I spent my whole life running away from something. I did not realize it was God until I met His Son, Jesus Christ, in the Los Angeles County Jail during Thanksgiving weekend, 1989.

I was running from the Texas Parole Board System I was hooked on heroin, cocaine and methadone. My self-esteem was at an all-time low and I couldn't go any lower, so I looked up and called on the Lord. I told the Lord that I do not know how to pray. The Lord took all of my fears away and broke my addiction. I never suffered any pain! That is when I knew that the Lord was real. I had gone "cold-turkey" with my addiction many times before, but when I called on the Lord, a definite change came. My life has not been the same since then.

Therefore, every pathway that is blocked by a door must be opened in prayer. Prayer is the key and faith unlocks the door. We have to always be willing to give someone, anyone, the right hand of fellowship whenever they are asking for help (Acts 3:7). You don't know when someone is going to be changed, but you can make sure that when they do, you will know that you had a helping hand in the "lost being found". We have to be about the Lord's business.

In the Los Angeles county jail, they kept transferring you from jail to jail to keep us away from our families until they could build their case. It took 3 weeks for my lady friend to find out where I was. And I told her to go back home because she didn't know anyone in Los Angeles. And then they expedited me back to Texas. It was ironic because I was escorted by two police and the other guy they were picking up from jail only had one police. And I asked the officer why are there two on me and one on the other guy and they told me that I was known as armed and dangerous.

After that when I came back to Texas, to start doing my time again, I started studying the Bible with the brotherhood of St. Andrews Episcopal Church. I started fellowshipping with them and reading the Bible. I started praying in the group of men and I prayed to the Lord and said that I would try you for 90 days. At four months they woke me up and told me that I had made my parole. There were 33 of us that were paroled. I was handcuffed to this Hispanic guy and we began talking, After talking for a while, he said, "I like you, Billy, and when you get settled I want you to come to Juarez and I will give you a kilo of heroin that you can cut ten times". I started thinking about 10 kilos of heroin that I could take back to Austin and be a king. When we got back to Huntsville, they only called 32 names for parole release. I asked why my name wasn't called and was told I had a protest in Austin, so I had to go back to the transit dorm. As I was walking back, the Lord spoke to me and told me that I was not going out yet because I was not ready for the streets;

I want you to stay a little while longer and get to know me better. I went back and prayed and asked the Lord to forgive me and told the Lord that if this is my destiny to spend the rest of my life in prison, I would accept it and serve Him. I went back to my unit and began studying and praying. About six months later they came and woke me up again and told me I had a parole interview.

In the interview the parole officer asked me what it would take for me to stay out of prison. I said the Lord Jesus Christ would keep me out of prison, but he said that I didn't want to hear that. I told him that I don't care what you want to hear, but the lord will keep me out of prison. I must stay with the Lord and learn of Him and that is what will keep me and help me stay out of prison. He looked through my file and closed it and said he was going to let me go home. I asked him about the protest and he opened the book and closed it and said do not worry about the protest. Then he said if he ever caught me on the streets in Austin, he would run me over. I told him that if he saw me on the streets, I would be witnessing. I left prison on December 5, 1990, to go home. I took everything I had from prison with me this time, including my Bible and literature. I went home and stayed with my mom and went to church with her. I joined my mom's church and while I was in orientation I was giving the teacher my witnessing testimony and he told me it was best not to say anything about that. I ended up leaving that church, it did not work out because of the orientation incident. So I left there and went to The Right Way Missionary Baptist Church. We didn't have the same view. You have to change your attitude but not your perspective.

I met my spiritual father at the time and he invited me to come to his church, they were having revival that week. I went and joined that church during the revival and I started doing street ministry again. I met the Pastor's son and we started running and hanging out, doing street ministry and that kept me busy. I started doing ministry in the prisons and nursing homes. If it had not been for my spiritual father's son, I would have left the church for good. He encouraged me to hang in there and stay faithful to God's Word. I stayed at The Right Way for about three years.

I took some time off from work to go back to California, to go look for my lady friend and go visit my kids in California. I went looking for my lady friend, in Los Angeles and I happen to see a guy and asked him about my lady friend. I started sharing the gospel with him and he told me he had seen her once and that she was up in Hollywood. I went looking for her, and one guy said he knew her. He was taking me around to look for my lady friend. He was a dope fiend, so I had to fix him and get him high while trying to find her and every dope den we went by to look for her. I think everywhere we went, we ended up missing her. The next day I had to leave but before I left I made another attempt to find my lady friend before catching my flight I met another prostitute who knew where she was. I gave her my card to give to my lady friend, if she saw her. I had about $25 that I had to give the dope fiend and then I had to turn in the car. When I got on plane and I had a map from the rental car and I circled an area and ask the Lord to keep her safe because I knew that she was still alive. And I came back from California and went home and started training for anther marathon, and there was an earthquake in Los Angeles. I left home to go run a marathon in Houston when I came back home, I received a message from my lady friend saying that she came home from the earthquake. I eventually found her and bought her flowers and we sat down and talked. I told her I had gave my life to the Lord and thanked God for bringing her back home. I wanted to share Christ with her and I married her. When we got married and I took her to church with me. I got a lot feedback (unwanted) of she is not a preachers wife and that kind of wore her and me down and she couldn't take it anymore. I had took her through cold turkey, because she was still hooked on drugs, but we still had been going through negative experiences in the church. She wanted to go get some drugs and I didn't want to do that but ended up going to get her drugs to calm her down so we could talk. I tried to talk to her and let her know you can't listen to people, trying to minister to her and she wouldn't listen to it. I got some pills from my friend to help her. After 3 days, it did not work out, she left and I tried to minister to her from a distance. And that did not work out, so we got an annulment.

I recall I got discouraged about my fellowship there at The Right Way and started coming to St. John Missionary Baptist Church and that's I how I met my current Pastor. He would encourage me, when I would speak at various places, by telling me to just use my testimony. And under his guidance and leadership I became more confident in speaking. I joined St. John in 1994 and got baptized again under my current Pastor's teaching. I had gotten baptized as a kid, but I didn't have a lot of knowledge of what it meant. Afterwards, I began serving in the Prison ministry and Nursing home and became his Assistant.

Though we are saved and set apart, we have spiritual warfare that is our battle every day. It took me about 12 years to get into another relationship. And that is when I met my wife at St. John. She had two 15 year olds and a 12 year old. I learned the challenges of a blended family fast. When you get married everything changes from you dealing with others. The first part of our marriage was really challenging because

I wanted to raise them up in the fear and admonition of the Lord. We struggled early on, but we both overcame and came into agreement on honoring God. I had to learn a lot about my selfishness and the financial challenges of a relationship. After 90 days I wanted to get out of it, but didn't, to "save face" with the Lord, holding onto my faith in Him that he will do it because I had asked for a wife. I then tried to do the best I could. 3 years into my marriage, I preached a sermon at St. John in 2005 I used my combat experience and after the sermon a guy came up to me and told me that he could help me because he told me I had PTSD and he asked for some information from me. He made arrangements for me to start going to the VA to get treatment. That is how I found out I had PTSD from being in Vietnam. It helped me realize how much I was withdrawn from people. And between my childhood and my development or being withdrawn, I would not have known how to communicate better. We endured, our marriage, and we are still growing and learning.

I got involved with Pastor in the church and got a lot of feedback about his position over me and giving me responsibilities that he had not given others. God has given me the ability of discernment that I needed in both the world and the church about dealing with people. I got involved at St. John here and have been there for 24 years. And there have been a few people her that have given me words of encouragement that have helped me. I know that I have been a part of helping others and I try to encourage people to try to live right. And that is how we should live as Christians in walking in the love of God and showing our light to people and not being negative.

When I first got out of prison, I went to the Veterans Administration and I told them I had a problem in 1991. And I told my situation to the doctor about drug use and that I had been in and out of prison, 3 broken marriages and that I had a problem and he told me that I did not have any problems and that was in 1991. With me being just saved I took him at his word and I left it at that. After going back and forth to the doctor, I was finally diagnosed with PTSD in 2006. And that was a struggle with me now, dealing with the stress of my family and the PTSD. I deal with the stress by running and exercising.

I preached that sermon and God has blessed me by working with my doctors at the VA. The social worker helped me work through my issues. She made it possible for me to do research and find others that were with me in Vietnam. I also had the opportunity to meet others since I had been working with my VA Counselor.

I also visited Pete's grave last year. I am also going to visit a lieutenant that was from Austin who was actually buried in Austin, but had died that day with the others in Bravo Company. This all came about was from a guy here that supported us in the Missions 5k Run. He introduced me to the Honor Flight program and I was able to go to Washington, D. C. I was able to see Kenneth's name and that was very emotional for me to experience this because I did not know where Kenneth was because I was not saved then. I saw this black guy Marine there and shared with him how emotional it was for blacks back then. He told me that the military always shares the plan of Salvation with all military personnel. That gave me some comfort and a new commitment to run marathons as a memorial for my comrades.

A SAD STATE OF
BEING LOST

AFTER MANY YEARS OF using drugs and hiding from family members, my lifestyle had taken its final toll on my body. My mother came to Houston looking for me. I was living in the worst part of the city, Third Ward, Ennis, Elgin and Rosedale area. My body was rancid with sores and abscesses. My condition was so bad that it greatly shocked my mother. She had never seen me this way. When our eyes met, I heard her cry out to God. She said, "Lord, you take him! I can't handle it anymore." "You have to hold him up, Lord!" That night, she gave me to the Lord in prayer, left with tears in her eyes and never looked back. She loved me so much, that she let me go. This reminded me of the story of Hannah. Hannah gave her son, Samuel to the Lord (1 Samuel 1:11, 22). We are to cast all of our cares on Him, for He cares for us (1 Peter 5:7).

FAITH IS THE KEY

EVERYTHING THAT I DO is by faith. I had a job, but left it to follow the work that Jesus had for me. When I first got out of prison I did some yard work with a friend of my father who had his own business and while working with him and sharing my testimony with him he wanted to help. He had contact with a lady in the City of Austin and she got me a temp job working with the city doing yard work. After doing yard work, I got moved to a survey unit and worked with a crew of guys who did half the work and the other guys would go around looking at women, not doing any work. By me being saved, that did not interest me, so I would bow my head and pray in the back seat, they thought I was sleep. And they told me I couldn't be sleeping on the job and I told them I was not sleeping, I was praying. They reported me to internal affairs and I was asked why was I reported and I told them I didn't want to be doing what they were doing. So they transferred me out to a new plant and I had a chance to pray and study the Bible there. When I would signed up for prison ministry, I would have to take off on Fridays to go, and I got a lot of negative feedback because of that. While praying and meditating the Lord said to me, I took care of you and you didn't know me for 30 years, now you know me and don't trust me, where is your faith? He's my Boss!

Because of faith in Christ (John 14:12), I resigned from my job that year and the Lord has met all of my needs and I am confident that He will continue to do so until He calls my name. At the time I was renting my mom's house and when I stepped out on faith to go into full time ministry, I asked the Lord and told him there would be hell when I told my mom I was going into ministry full time. And my mom asked me how I was going to pay the rent and I told her the Lord will make a way. So I started paying my way, cutting yards and using my disability to pay rent for the house. One day the Lord gave a vision to my mother to restructure the house and rent part of the house out and build an efficiency to the house in the back for me.

When a person stands to testify as a witness to a particular situation, he can only speak of what he has seen or heard pertaining to that situation. Mine was the faith I had in God and the life experiences that he had been with me through all that I had been through, he would be with now. In my short time of ministry, I have heard a lot of "stuff" from Christians that is not biblical. As we focus on Dependency and Co-Dependency, we must realize that it is not us, or in another person on which we depend. Our dependency must be on the Lord. The real problem lies in our fears. Speaking for myself, I was dependent on drugs, I feared the pain of suffering from the withdrawal from not having those drugs available. It was the fear that drove me to continue using drugs. The same is true of co-dependency, it is fear of losing a loved one that keeps shadowed dreams alive. When parents try to help their children it can hinder their progress.

Drugs are a minor sin when compared to sexual perversions, fornication and adultery which involves another person. What enters a person does not defile, but what comes out is what defiles him (Mark 7:18-23). When we choose to do certain things that are contrary to sound doctrine, drastic consequences arise. No one ties a drug abuser down to abuse his/ her body; that is their decision. "Curiosity has always killed the cat". I can remember when I first started using drugs, I would drive older drug addicts around hustling and every time we came back from hustling we would go to Spanish town in Austin, to a house and they would leave me in the living room, while they went to the back. And when they came back their whole demeanor changed so I kept asking what they would be doing when they went back and just kept asking. So one day a guy named "Black Jack" gave me a hit and that is how it all started. One morning I felt like I had the flu and I went to him and told him what was going on with me and he gave me another fix, and this started my drug addiction. The world is full of curious youth as well as adults. Drugs have plagued every age group, young middle age, and old.

Parents are trying to hold on to their children whose destiny is in the hand of God. "The wicked are estranged from the womb; they go astray as soon as they are born speaking lies" (Psalm 58:3). God often shows us in His Word that even a child is known by his deeds, by whether the things that he does are pure and right(Proverbs 20:11). Without training, there is no hope!

REDEMPTION AND FORGIVENESS

REDEMPTION AND FORGIVENESS HAVE always run hand in hand between God and my mother. God knew that Jesus was my Redeemer and my mother's spirit of forgiveness would forever be apparent. I remember when my mother came to visit me in prison, I had just become born again. At the time I was real thin, from running in prison. She told me that she was getting too old to keep driving down from Austin to Houston and she couldn't keep coming down to visit because it was dangerous for her by herself. I told her not to worry anymore, I had given my life to Christ and I am in His hands. We talked for a little while and I could still see concern in her eyes. The next week she came back again and brought my brother with her; I never had two back to back visits before. They came to visit and check on me. I told them I was alright. My brother asked why I was so thin. I told him I was not sick. They thought I had AIDS. And I told them whatever I had, Jesus took it to the cross when He died for me. We had a good visit and they left. Redemption and forgiveness calls for communication. You have to be able to communicate with God and people. As previously stated, "Failure to communicate can cause an individual to grow indignant and confused." "Thank God for my mother!" She did all she could to bring me up right!

A SINNER'S STORY

THERE IS A SINNER'S story that draws my attention about Jesus. Luke 19:1-10 tells a story about a man named Zacchaeus. A rich man that was lost, but now found, simply because he wanted to see Jesus. All of us are lost and not found, blind and can't see, because of the desires of our hearts that are contrary to the Word of God. Zacchaeus realized that the Savior was coming through Jericho. Jericho is the great sinner's city that was cursed by Joshua after the walls came tumbling down (Joshua 6). Jericho, that great sinner's city, is where the New Testament records two events happening there when Jesus came through, the healing of the two blind men and the saving and conversion of Zacchaeus' soul. The story opens as Jesus is entering and passing through Jericho. He is not intending to stop, but just passing through. Now, at some point in our lives, all of us who are born again believers are passing through a Jericho. Some of us will get lost in the city, while others will be found by the Savior. Many are called, but few are chosen. I heard blind Bartimeus cry out in Jericho: "Jesus, the Son of David, have mercy on me". And the Lord heard and called him to himself. Just as Jesus heard him, He also knew Zacchaeus, the chief tax collector would be found in Jericho. Paul reminded Timothy through his testimony, "This is a faithful saying, and worthy of all acceptance that Christ Jesus came into the world to save sinners, of whom I am chief" (1 Timothy 1:15). Zacchaeus was a chief sinner, who was no ordinary tax collector. He was rich but unhappy. Money can get you the best doctors in town, the best lawyers, and the best husband or wife and yet all of these things are null and void in your life without the peace of God which passes all understanding. Zacchaeus sought to see Jesus but because of a pressing crowd, he was unable. So he ran ahead and climbed up into a sycamore tree and that is what it takes to get to where Jesus can see your act of faith. Your faith is not based upon the crowd around you, but on your determination to stay in the presence of the Lord. People may give you a strange look, but to be determined means to stay ahead and remain in the race and when Jesus sees you, He will say: "Servant, make haste and come down, for today I must stay at your house."

The principle thought here is that when you sincerely desire to see Jesus, you must be willing to go through pains and not be ashamed to take advantage of the opportunity to represent Him. Great will be your reward, "for He is a rewarder of those who diligently seek Him." Zacchaeus' reward was two-fold. Jesus invited Himself and the place of their entertainment was at the home of Zacchaeus. He also called Zacchaeus by name; Christ knows His chosen by name. Are they not written in the Lamb's Book of Life? It is a great honor to be chosen by God to represent Christ in this life.

"No man can come to me, except the Father which hath sent me draw him and I will raise him up at the last day."

(John 6:44) He looks beyond our unworthiness to satisfy our needs. Our needs are to recognize that we have an adversary which is the devil and his desires is to kill us with things such as abortions and if he misses you through abortions, he try to kill us though our struggles and fights that we are not aware of. We are to live joyful lives because God knows that our lives were predestined from our mother's womb (Jeremiah 1: 4-5). When we become saved and study the Word of God, then we know that problems are not with flesh and blood but in heavenly places. One way or another the devil has been trying to kill me through shoot outs, overdose, war in Vietnam, and in the streets. So once we become aware who our enemy is then we can win the fight of faith. Just like the story of Zacchaeus did as he deceived many. Jesus brings the party with Him because we are rejoicing now that we are saved and can rejoice in him because he is with us in the spirit. We looked to the Lord because he is our battle ax; He is our everything. We do not have Jesus in the flesh to entertain us in our house today, but we have His disciples and fellowship in Christian love and we must treat everyone as they were Jesus, even our enemies.

BE EVER ALERT

THE GREATEST VERSE IN the story of Zacchaeus is verse 7. Whenever people see you doing something that they should be doing, they start nagging, murmuring and criticizing you. They accused Jesus of associating with sinners. Jesus tells us that if they would persecute Him, they will also persecute you. If they keep my Word, they will keep your Word. Isn't it strange how people who are in church often treat new converts the way they do? I made a vow to the Lord that I would do three things daily that would keep me focused and stable:

1.) Study the Bible, prayerfully;

2.) Stay involved in the works of the church; and

3.) Share my testimony, whenever and wherever possible.

Sadly to say, my former orientation teacher told me to keep quiet about my testimony. I didn't stay there too long afterwards because at that time, all that I had was a sound testimony. I had only been saved for one year. All that I knew was where I came from, and where I was going. For, Zacchaeus told the Lord, "I will give half of my goods to the poor and if I have taken anything from anyone by false accusation, I will restore them four fold".

True repentance will always make you give back to society and to people whatever you have secured dishonestly and Zacchaeus knew that he had made some cunning deals with the people, but he realized that he was in the presence of the Lord. Coming unto Jesus, confession and truth is eminent for Jesus said salvation has come to this house, for the Son of Man seeks and saves that which is lost!

I WILL GIVE IT
BACK LORD

IN LUKE 19:3, ZACCHAEUS wanted to see who Jesus was. Now he may have heard about Jesus using the parable of the Pharisees and the Tax Collector in Luke Chapter 18. The tax collector was justified for his humbleness and the Pharisee was not because of his pride. Zacchaeus could not see Jesus because of his height or stature and the crowd. If you do not love your neighbor as yourself, you will forever be in short stature in this life. Paul says, "If it is possible, as much as depends on you, live peaceably with all men" (Romans 12:18). Zacchaeus was not living peaceably as so are many Christians are not living peaceably today.

In verse 4, weeping may have endured for a while for Zacchaeus' life, but this did not stop him from wanting to see Jesus, thus, he climbed the tree. Many of the problems of today lie in the fact that we refuse to "climb" above our problems, but chose rather to remain and "wallow" in them. Zacchaeus was determined!

Through determination, we hear the Lord's Prayer in Luke 19: 5, when Jesus came to where Zacchaeus was. Jesus lifted up His eyes and prayed, "Father, the hour has come, glorify your Son, that your Son may also glorify you" (John 17:1). Determination places us on the Lord's Prayer list. We know that it does not matter how hard we try to make haste and welcome the Lord's presence in our home, within our family and to our friends. The Bible tells us that there will always be an enemy in the camp, the devil and some envious, jealous spirit lurking in the house.

That is why Zacchaeus was not ashamed to admit before the Lord as well as before his friends about the life that he had been living, because when you are standing before the master of Truth, the Lord, you will have to tell the truth. "For the Word of God is sharper than a two-edged sword" (Hebrews 4:12). I promised the Lord that I would give Him my time, my talent, and my all. I would surrender to be used for His glory. That is why Jesus recognized Zacchaeus as a son of Abraham, because he gave back. Don't you know that it is more blessed to give than to receive? If you give God your heart in Faith, nothing will be impossible. "For with the heart, one believes to righteousness, and with the mouth confession is made to salvation" (Romans 10:19).

Jesus says today is Salvation spoken 2000 years ago in Jericho and is the same today. "But the Word is near you, even in your mouth and in your heart (that is the word of faith we preach), Romans 10:8.

RUNNING THE RACE
SUCCESSFULLY

I AM A DEDICATED marathon runner and have run over 60 marathons, with my best time of 3 hours and 6 seconds at 45 years old. I ran four Boston Marathons from 1994-1998. I am a Vietnam decorated Purple Heart Veteran who once struggled with many things since Vietnam. With all the years I have spent in prison, it is there that I started running. And while in prison, a guard saw me running on the yard one day and said that he thought that I could be a good marathon runner. So I prayed to the Lord and asked Him to let me run marathons, to be a witness to Him, sharing how God saved me and put running in my feet, instead of drugs in my arms.

There are three points to consider in running this race successfully:

1. You must finish the race. This means that you must look unto Jesus, who is the Author and Finisher of our faith. Zacchaeus knew that he had to lay

aside every weight and the sin, which so easily ensnares him, and run with endurance the race that was set before him, if he wanted to see Jesus. The question is: "Are you ready to lay aside every heavy load or weight that is burdening you? Such things as "foolish talking, course jesting, etc. or anything that is unfitting for saints, should be laid aside and rather giving thanks", Ephesians 5:4. For if God who spoke light into existence can be light, why not His only begotten Son who is light, draw all who are led by the light. Jesus says, "Ye are the light of the world. A city that is set on a hill cannot be hidden, Matthew 5:14. You must finish the race! It does not matter how you finish, but just keep moving forward and upward and one day you will see Jesus at the finish line sitting on the throne of Grace and Mercy

2. You must realize that you are not in the race alone. We, the believers of Christ, Jesus have an anchor on which we can depend on Him in our minds and in our spirit which will continuously secure our soul. The writer of Hebrews tells us, "This hope we have as an anchor of the soul, both sure and steadfast", Hebrews 6:19. To be personal for a moment, I began running in prison to pass the time away. Sometimes I would run for an hour and a half around the little court to run 28 times to be equivalent to a mile. I had never heard of marathon runners, but drugs I knew, 400 meters, and 200 meters, I did know! One day while running and prayer, I asked the Lord if he would allow me to run marathons as a testimony to His amazing

grace. God answers prayers! I was paroled on December 5, 1990 and on January 20, 1991. I ran in the Houston Marathon. The farthest I ever ran was 12 or 13 miles. I only had 54 days to grow my faith for the 26.2 mile run. I was training pretty well and my mother was my dietician and support so I found out that you could win a Mercedes running in the New York Marathon and I told my mom that I would win to get her that Mercedes. Then I went to Houston to run the first marathon, I didn't get the Mercedes but I did finished the race, but not before hitting the famous wall of marathoning at mile 22. My body system said stop. I could feel muscle spasms, pain of every description from head to toe. Right then and there, I said to the Lord, "Lord, I have been a failure all of my life, and it seems like I may fail this too". I could barely move my feet, so I started walking toward the finish line and after approximately 100 steps, I heard the spirit of the Lord say, "Move"! I began shoveling my feet, then the spirit said, "Run"! And I ran like a new creation. To date, I have run in more than 50 marathons including two 50-mile runs. Praise the Lord! We have to know that we have an anchor. "You are of God, little children, and have overcome the world, because He who is in you is greater than he who is in the world", 1 John 4:4. Jesus is at the finish line, sitting and waiting for us to come unto him.

3. Last and foremost, there is salvation at the finish line. Now you may say, "Well, Preacher, I have salvation now and I don't need to wait until I get

to the finish line". But we must be reminded that "we are a sinner, saved by grace for deliverance from the power of sin on the day of redemption, and Christ is our Redeemer". We still have to get there.

SALVATION THROUGH CHRIST JESUS

THE SALVATION THAT COMES through Christ may be described in three tenses, past, present…and future. When we believe in Christ, we are saved, Acts 16:31. But we are also in the process of being saved from the power of sin, Romans 7:13 and Philippians 2:12. Finally, we shall be saved from the very presence of sin, Romans 13:11 and Titus 2:12-13. Until then, God only releases into our lives the power of Christ's resurrection, Romans 6:4. …and allows us a foretaste of our future life as His children, 2 Corinthians 1:22 and Ephesians 1:14. But only at the finish line will things be complete for our salvation, Hebrews 9:28. Even though the finish line is far off, we must continuously embrace the promise of God, confess our faith and believe that we are strangers and pilgrims on this earth. Jesus says, "Heaven and Earth might pass away, but my Word stands forever".

AREAS FOR HEALTHY COMMUNICATION

THE FOLLOWING ARE AREAS for healthy communication within families, neighbors and the church:

1. You have to be saved first and if you are not, it is very necessary that you DO IT NOW. Ask Jesus to come into your heart right now!

2. There must be proof in your life. Our proof is recorded in the Bible. We are the only Bible that the non-believer often reads.

3. Always be willing to share your past to brighten the future of those who are lost. You may help them to find their way to Christ Jesus.

HIS WORD MINISTRY – THE BEGINNING

NOW FOR THE BEGINNING there must be a title to draw substance from; to shape, form and complete a work of delight. In this letter I wish to start from the beginning not so much as the beginning of the books in the Bible, from Genesis to Revelation, but from the beginning of the Gospel of John, where we are moved from the beginning of the creation of the world in Genesis to the eternity of God in John.

"In the beginning was the Word, and the Word was with God, and the Word was God. He was in the beginning with God" (John 1:1-2). In the beginning was the Word, but where did the Word come from? Did it come from space, another planet in our solar system, or did the wind blow the Word in to existence. No, I believe and hope that you agree that the Word came from God. If we are in time and time has a beginning, the Word must have existed before time began. In the book of John, in verse 14 he writes, "the Word became flesh and dwelt among us, and we beheld His glory, the glory as of the only begotten of the Father, full of grace and truth." Verses 1 and 14 clearly state that Jesus was present with God in the beginning because Jesus is the Word of God in the flesh. 1 John 4:2-3 states, "By this you know the spirit of God; every spirit that confesses that Jesus Christ has come in the flesh is of God and every spirit that does not confess that Jesus Christ has come in the flesh is not of God." Furthermore verse 1 goes on to say, "And the Word was with God". Verse 18 says, "No one has seen God at any time". John clearly writes this to emphasize a key word in his gospel, "You Must Believe".

Belief is the apex of John's gospel. John states, "Believe in what I am saying because I have been with Jesus. I have heard the thunder roar; I have seen the lightning flash; I have eaten with Jesus; I have slept with Jesus; I have laughed and talked with Jesus; and I have seen God because I have seen Jesus". John 14:9 says, "Jesus said to him, have I been with you so long and yet you have not known me, Philip? He who has seen me has seen the Father."

Even from Jesus' fleshly state, he was with God, and we can also be with God, through His Holy Spirit, who comes in to our lives daily with resurrection power from Christ Jesus. Jesus is our Word from God by His spirit. It is the spirit that gives life; the flesh profits nothing (John 6:63). Just imagine God stepping out of glory for you and me. That is something to shout about! Hallelujah and Praise the Lord!

James 4:7-8 says, "Submit to God, resist the devil and he will flee from you. Draw near to God and He will draw near to you. Cleanse your hands, you sinners; and purify your hearts you double-minded. Going down memory lane really gives me an opportunity to share the pieces of the puzzle that God has completed in me through the blood of Jesus Christ. You do know that we become the righteousness of God in

Him (2 Corinthians 5:21). Continuing down memory lane, I look at "Madness that Turned Sour". In Ephesians 4:26-27, Paul says, "be angry and do not sin, do not let the sun go down on your wrath, nor give place to the devil." According to the Word of God, it is okay to become angry and get upset, but do not let it drive you to sin. As I look back over my life, I am reminded of a movie I once saw called "Cool Hand Luke", staring Paul Newman. The apex of the movie was the statement quote, "failure to communicate". He did not know how to communicate with the prison guard and the guard did not care to communicate with him. The guard knew that if he could keep him in the state-of-mind that he was in, there would not be anything to worry about. Satan, the devil, wanted to keep me in that same state of mentality, confined but not for communication purposes.

As I stated before, failure to communicate can cause a person to grow indignant and confused. I grew up in a single parent home. My dad left when I was young, but my mother was God-fearing woman who held on to her faith and endured the challenges before her and pressed on. I grew up looking for a father or brother figure. Even though I was molested, I know it could have been worse for me. I could have turned out gay. But Psalms 8:2 declares, "Out of the mouth of babes and infants you have ordained strength, because of your enemies, that you may silence the enemy and the avenger". My failure to communicate left me in the hands of a praying mother, and a big brother from my dad's previous marriage who also lived in the projects. The molestation stopped when the news of my brother was known. I did not know why it stopped until years later when I preached my first sermon and gave my testimony. My big brother called me that evening, after preaching my sermon, and mentioned the name of the guy who molested me. All I could say was, "Praise the Lord".

Years passed and I witnessed this same act my homeboys were doing to another child. Being hit with reality, I knew this act of indecency was wrong. I became angry at that man because he robbed me of my innocence and that is when I took a blood oath that no one would every hurt me again. My whole life changed right then and there.

Failure to communicate had already taken its toll on me, so whatever came my way, I felt I could handle it. I was 37 years old when I told my brother about the molestation. Three years later, I told my mother. In all those years, I wondered what I would do if I saw the man that molested me. James 4:8 states, "draw near to God and He will draw near to you". In the world, you hear all kinds of axioms. All of my life I felt unclean and unworthy until I came to know the Lord Jesus. Only after being called out of darkness did that man who molested me, come to me for a testimony. I told him that what he did was wrong, but I do not hold anything against him. He was still lost (unsaved), so he fled from me. Resist the devil and he will flee from you. Praise the Lord!

Conclusion

With thanksgiving in my heart for my deliverance, it is my sincere hope, desire and prayer that my story will be a blessing to you, your families, your neighbors and the church, the body of Christ. And that it will inspire those who have lost their way to realize and believe that they too can be found through belief, faith, hope and trust in our Lord and Savior, Jesus Christ.

GOD BELSS YOU!

About the Author

PREACHER BILLY LEE'S BACKGROUND is an "on hands" educational experience that began during his childhood. He graduated from the "University of Hard Knocks", becoming a high school dropout and receiving a degree in "abuse and deception".

He then entered the armed forces of the United States Marine Corp and is a Vietnam Veteran. He received the Nation's Defense Medal, the Vietnamese Service Medal, the Vietnamese Campaign Medal, and three Purple Heart Medals and received an Honorable Discharge in 1970.

With determination, he received his certificate of High School equivalency at Texas Southern University of Houston in 1974, also completing two semesters of higher learning as well. Later, he received an Associate of Arts Degree from Alvin Community College in 1983 and 14 credit hours of study from the University of Houston at Clear Lake. He also has a background in theological studies from the Southwest Episcopal Seminary.

After being released from prison on December 5, 1990, he announced his call into the ministry on March 28, 1993.

He received a Certificate of Ordination, November 18, 1994. His current membership is with St. John Missionary Baptist Church, where he serves as Pastoral Care Minister and serves as an evangelist in the prisons, nursing homes and in the street ministry. He continues to visit Travis County jails, sharing the Word of God.

❦

To LEARN MORE ABOUT Drug and Alcohol Addiction, Drug Dependence and Veterans and Post Traumatic Stress Disorder (PTSD), please visit the National Council on Alcoholism and Drug Dependence, Inc. (NCADD): https://www.ncadd.org/ or call the Hope Line at 1-800-622-2255.

Printed in the United States
By Bookmasters